C000263739

Brian Patten was born in Liverpo[...]
his poems have been publishe[...]
Little Johnny's Confession, No[...]
Irrelevant Song, Vanishing Tric[...]
Storm Damage. The poems contained in *Grinning Jack* are
drawn from the first five of these volumes.

Patten also writes for younger readers. His novel, *Mr Moon's
Last Case* won a special award from the Mystery Writers of
America and received critical acclaim on both sides of the
Atlantic. With collections of verse such as *Gargling With Jelly*,
he is one of our best loved poets for children.

Also by Brian Patten

Love Poems
Storm Damage

Children's Books

The Elephant and the Flower
Jumping Mouse
Emma's Doll
Mr Moon's Last Case
Gargling With Jelly
Jimmy Tag-along

Author's Note

A few of the earliest of these poems were written when I was
fifteen or sixteen and perhaps ought to have been relegated to
juvenilia, but the boy who wrote them would have argued quite
vehemently (if not quite accurately) that his poems were as
good as many by older poets. As I haven't the heart to dissuade
him, I've slipped a few in. I've not included any of my love
poems here as they are available in a separate collection. Any
minor changes in these poems are changes that have evolved
through reading in performance. With a few exceptions, the
poems are arranged in chronological order.

GRINNING JACK
Selected Poems

Brian Patten

UNWIN
PAPERBACKS

LONDON SYDNEY WELLINGTON

First published in Great Britain by Unwin Paperbacks, an imprint
of Unwin Hyman Limited in 1990

UNWIN HYMAN LIMITED
15–17 Broadwick Street, London W1V 1FP

Allen & Unwin Australia Pty Ltd
8 Napier Street, North Sydney, NSW 2060, Australia

Allen & Unwin New Zealand Pty Ltd with the Port Nicholson Press
Compusales Building, 75 Ghuznee Street, Wellington, New Zealand

Cataloguing in Publication Data applied for

ISBN 0-04-440-6096

Printed and bound in Great Britain
by Cox & Wyman Ltd, Reading

Contents

Little Johnny's confession 9
Johnny learns the language 10
Little Johnny's change of personality 11
Little Johnny's foolish invention 12
Little Johnny's night visitor 14
Little Johnny's final letter 15
Little Johnny takes a trip to another planet 16
Ah Johnny, what when you're older? 17
Where are you now, Batman? 18
A theme for various murders 19
Schoolboy 21
Without knowing much about it 24
Sleep now 25
Room 26
Come into the city Maud 28
After breakfast 30
Prose poem towards a definition of itself 32
The beast 33
A talk with a wood 34
The projectionist's nightmare 35
Sad Adam 36
The prophet's good idea 38
Through the tall grass in your head 40
Having taken the necessary precautions 41
The song 42
Portrait of a young girl raped at a suburban party 43
Note to the hurrying man 44
Note while walking home 45
Genesis 46
School note 47
Seen through the trees behind which you're walking 48
Mr Jones takes over 49

The telephonists   50
The lyric bird   52
The pint-sized Ark   54
You'd better believe him   55
Old crock   56
Ode on celestial music   58
The necessary slaughter   59
The irrelevant song   60
Interruption at the opera house   66
Spring song   68
Cosmic misery   69
The unicorn   70
Albatross ramble   71
It's selfish to be happy, say the gloomy   74
The main character   75
The literary gathering   76
The giant seen   77
Travelling between places   78
The obsolete nightingale   79
'If you had to hazard a guess'   85
Nursery rhyme for the sleepless   86
After frost   87
Believing in the wall   88
Night piece   89
Winter note   90
Hopeful   91
Waves   91
In the high-rise Alice dreams of Wonderland   92
Meat   93
The wrong number   96
I studied telephones constantly   97
Turning the pages   101
I tried to find my voice   102
Blake's purest daughter   104
Pipe dream   106

Drunk	107
Conversation with a favourite enemy	110
Proclamation from the new Ministry of Culture	111
Ghost-culture	112
John Poole's bullying the angels	113
A bird-brained view of power	114
The critics' chorus	116
The common denominator	118
Brer Rabbit's Howler	119
Brer Rabbit in the market place	120
Brer Rabbit's revenge	121
Brer Rabbit at the ants' banquet	122
Note from the laboratory assistant's notebook	124
Staring at the crowd	125
Song of the grateful char	126
The right mask	128
Going back and going on	130
One reason for sympathy	131
The last gift	132
Advice from the original gatecrasher to the recently dead	134
The purpose is ecstasy	135
Assembling a prayer	136
Friends	138
Something never lost	139
The mule's favourite dream	140
Song about home	141
Frogs in the wood	142

Little Johnny's confession

THIS MORNING
       being rather young and foolish
    I borrowed a machinegun my father
    had left hidden since the war, went out,
    and eliminated a number of small enemies.
    Since then I have not returned home.

This morning
       swarms of police with trackerdogs
       wander about the city
       with my description printed
       on their minds, asking:
       'Have you seen him?
       He is seven years old,
       likes Pluto, Mighty Mouse
       and Biffo the Bear,
       have you seen him, anywhere?'

This morning
       sitting alone in a strange playground
       muttering you've blundered, you've blundered
       over and over to myself
       I work out my next move
       but cannot move.
       The trackerdogs will sniff me out,
       they have my lollypops.

Johnny learns the language

Yesterday
   in order to explain myself
I locked myself away
with an old alphabet,
with the hand-me-down phrases for which
I had no use but to which
I was already addicted.

Yesterday,
   while considering how absurd it was
   that everything has a name
   I discovered that the mayfly
   was weighed down by a single vowel.
   Under the threat of not being understood
   I began to understand
   how words were the nets in which
   what I was floundered.

Mother,
   you come with your bowl of words,
   fat words, puffed with kindness.
   And father
   you come with your silences in which
   words sneak about like thieves.

   I am learning your language.
   'Loss' 'Defeat' 'Regret'—
   Without understanding
   You would have these be
   the blueprints for my future.

Little Johnny's change of personality

THIS AFTERNOON
    While looking for hidden meanings in Superman
And discussing tadpole collections
I discovered I belonged to Generation X
And developed numerous complexes;
I turned on to Gothic fairytales and Aleister Crowley,
Began to question your authority, so

Please Mr Teacher, Sir,
Turn round from your blackboard,
The whole class has its hands up,
We're in rather a hurry.
The desks are returning to forests,
The inkwells are overflowing,
The boys in the backrow have drowned.
Please Mr Teacher, Sir,
Turn round from your blackboard,
Your chalks are crumbling,
Your cane's decaying,
Turn round from your blackboard
We're thinking of leaving.

This afternoon
    A quiet criminal moves through the classroom
Deciding on his future;
Around him, things have fallen apart—
Something's placed an inkstained finger
On his heart.

Little Johnny's foolish invention

A Fable for Atomic Adam

ONE DAY
   while playing with old junk in the attic
Little Johnny accidentally invented an atomic bomb
and not knowing what to do with it
buried it in the front garden.

Next morning
   during cornflakes and sunrise
   he noticed it glowing damp among the cabbages
   and so took it out
   out into the city
   where it smelt of tulips
   but was sadly inedible.

What can I do with it, he sighed, having nowhere to hide it?
I'm afraid that soon a busy policeman might come along
to detain me, I'd make a statement. Say,

         I'd like a new bomb, a blue bomb,
a fizzy-drink and an ice-cream bomb,
a bomb I could explode in rooms
where my friends are sleeping,
that would not wake them or shake them but
would keep them from weeping;
         a bomb I could bounce in the playground
and spray over flowers, a bomb
that would light the Universe for years.

But he'd pay no attention he
would simply take out his notebook and write:
This child is mad.
This child is a bomb.

Last night in my nightmares
my foolish invention became transparent
and through it my atomic friends wandered, naked
but for a few carefully placed leaves
that were continually rotting.

So now carrying a megaton of regrets
I trace about obscure cities
looking for a place to leave my bomb
but am always turned away by minor officials
who say, 'It's a deterrent,' and I answer, Sure
It will evaporate milk from the lips of dreaming children,

It will deter
flower and bird and sunlight from calling
and one morning
at sunrise when I rise and glow
I'll look outside to make certain my invention has not
                                                blossomed
but will see nothing through
the melting windows.

Little Johnny's night visitor

LAST NIGHT,
　　before sleep ambushed me,
　the bogey-man came.
　He limped up the stairs,
　stood on the landing,
　whispered my name.

I pretended not to hear him.
　I conjured up some heros.
　I was invisible.
　I was bullet-proof.
　I could fly away from him,
　leap out the window, leap
　across the rooftops to escape him.

Last night
　I heard him try the door of my bedroom.
　I heard him cross the room.
　I locked the sheets,
　I made the bed into iron.
　I made myself so tiny he could not find me.

Last night,
　before sleep could rescue me,
　the bogey-man came.
　Drunk, he stumbled over words
　he will never repeat again.

Father,
　please do not stare at me.
　Do not come so close.
　I do not know how to love strangers.

Little Johnny's final letter

MOTHER,
I won't be home this evening, so
don't worry; don't hurry to report me missing.
Don't drain the canals to find me,
I've decided to stay alive, don't
search the woods, I'm not hiding,
simply gone to get myself classified.
Don't leave my shreddies out,
I've done with security.
Don't circulate my photograph to society
I have disguised myself as a man
and am giving priority to obscurity.
It suits me fine;
I have taken off my short trousers
and put on long ones, and
now am going out into the city, so
don't worry; don't hurry to report me missing.

I've rented a room without any curtains
and sit behind the windows growing cold;
heard your plea on the radio this morning,
you sounded sad and strangely old.

Little Johnny takes a trip to another planet

THROUGH HIS bedroom window, later they confirmed
Johnny drifted one Monday evening
Up above the sleeping world.

He left this message:

I've taken a trip to another planet
And I'll be away for a while,
Don't send the Escaped Children Squad after me,
the Universe is too wild.

Now among black glass trees
he weaves intricate shapes
in a world an inch away from ours,
and from behind his eyes
he sees into a waiting room of light
and maps out the route dawn takes through
the nurseries of night.

He has switched on a world and walked inside;
and as silence blooms among the flowers
he wonders at people groping
through transparent hours.
He's found the perfect loophole:
sits on the other side,
a child with eyes as big as planets
whose dreams do not collide
with any forms of teaching
with any form of lies.

So don't send the Escaped Children Squad after him
he'll be away for a while,
he's taken a trip to another planet
and the Universe is too wild
for him to make it back
in the same state of mind.

Ah Johnny, what when you're older?

AH JOHNNY,
What when you are older?
The Humphrey Bogart of Innocence
Wandering gangster fashion through your dreams?
What fantasies will you have
When finding Alice in some sunny glade
She lies down and says
'OK, Let's make it'.

Johnny will you still be sane when Winnie the Pooh
Grows into some gigantic bear
And comes to maul you?
When Noddy murders Big Ears,
When Archie attacks Mehitabel,
When Mr Toad finally crashes and Toad Hall perishes
With only the willows as witnesses?

When Brer Rabbit commits harikari inside a decaying tree-trunk
Will you report the incident
Or simply shrug your shoulders and wander away?

You'll find no magic potions, no strange herbs,
No bodies blushing with light—You'll grow podgy!
Buttoned up to the neck with respectability!
Already you're wearing pin-striped shirts! Bright shining shoes!
Johnny this is my last poem about you,
I'm afraid to remember what you were.
You'll find nothing when you've grown,
When all your routines are firmly established,
When the last young thigh you'll ever encounter
Turns round and machineguns you down.

Soon you will climb into a bus full of schoolchildren
And asking for a single back to innocence
Will collapse among the used tickets
Groaning some unintelligible ode nobody will remember.

Where are you now, Batman?

WHERE ARE you now, Batman? Now that Aunt Heriot has
      reported Robin missing
And Superman's fallen asleep in the sixpenny childhood
      seats?
Where are you now that Captain Marvel's SHAZAM! echoes
      round the auditorium?
The magicians don't hear, must all be deaf . . . or dead . . .
The Purple Monster who came down from The Purple Planet
      disguised as a man
Is wandering aimlessly about the streets
With no way of getting back;
Sir Galahad's been strangled by the Incredible Living Trees,
Zorro killed by his own sword.
In the junk-ridden, disused hangers
Blackhawk's buried the last of his companions;
Rocket Man's fuel tanks have given out over London.
Though the Monster and the Ape still fight it out
In a room where the walls are continually closing
No one is watching.
Even Flash Gordon's been abandoned,
A star-wanderer weeping over robots loved
            half a universe ago.

My celluloid companions, it's only a few years
Since I first knew you, yet already something in us had faded.
Did we kill you off simply by growing up?
We who made you possible with our unsophisticated minds
And with our pocket-money
And the sixpences we received for pretending to be good?
   Sucked from tiny terraces on Saturday mornings
We cheered you on from disaster to disaster,

Never imagining how that Terrible Fiend,
         that Ghastly Adversary
Mr Old Age, would catch you in his deadly trap
And come finally to polish you off,
His machine-gun dripping with years.

A theme for various murders

S HE WALKS alone by the river
     her adolescent breasts
   and eyes
      and hips
         and legs as well
that were once so cool around her schoolboy lover
   now move in time to dreams of her body's gangster
      waiting naked for her
         in a place where it is silent
            except for the downpour.

Lately she has become aware
   of her own movements;
      next to her body
         she wears very little;
She has heard of the freedom that like rain
   runs loose about the city
      —and being no different than her age,
         being only her age,
         she lies open to new possibilities
   and quick, new birds twitter in her blood.

But
    the gangster
       will dullen her,
          and he who will disappear eventually
            will cloud her innocence
   and we will find her only
      when all that's precious
         is dead in her.

Where is
   the schoolboy lover,
      tell me
         where is he?

Not down by that river
   but minute among his fantasies
      with potent secretaries
         who rise at dawn from his mind,
           damp and warm.
              and come out of his eyes

while she walks there
   alone this evening,
while she walks
   with the last crazy song
about to die in her.

Schoolboy

BEFORE PLAYTIME let us consider the possibilities
of getting stoned on milk.

      In his dreams,
scribbling overcharged on woodbines,
mumbling obscure sentences into his desk
'No way of getting out,
no way out. . . .'

      Poet dying of
too much education, schoolgirls, examinations,
canes that walk the nurseries of his wet dreams;
satchels full of chewing gum; bad jokes, pencils;
crude drawings performed in the name of art. Soon will
come the Joyful Realisation in Mary's back kitchen
    while mother's out.
All this during chemistry.

(The headmaster's crying in his study.
His old pinstriped pants rolled up to his knees
in a vain attempt to recapture youth; emotions
skid along his slippery age; Love, smeared across his face,
like a road accident.)

The schoolyard's full of people to hate.
Full of tick and prefects and a fat schoolmaster
and whistles and older and younger boys, but
he's growing
    sadly
        growing
           up.

Girls,
  becoming mysterious, are now more important
than arriving at school late or receiving trivial awards.
Photographs of those huge women
            seem a little more believable now.

(Secretly, the pale, unmarried headmaster telling him
Death is the only grammatically correct full-

                                    stop.)

Girls, still mysterious;
arithmetic thighed, breasts measured in thumbprints,
not inches.
Literature's just another way out.
History's full of absurd mistakes.
King Arthur if he ever existed
would only have farted and excused himself
from the Round Table in a hurry.

(The headmaster, staring through the study window
into the playground, composes evil poems about
the lyrical boy in class four)
            'He invited us up sir,
          but not for the cane,
              said the algebra of life
                was too difficult to explain
                  and that all equations
                    mounted to nothing . . .'

Growing up's wonderful if
                you keep your eyes closed tightly,
                and, if you manage to grow,
                take your soul with you,
                    nobody wants it.

So, playtime's finished with;
It's time to fathom out too many things:
To learn he's got a different authority watching over him.
The teacher gives way to the police,
Detention gives way to the prison.

He's going to learn strange things, learn
how to lie correctly, how to cheat and steal
        (in the nicest possible manner).
He will learn, amongst other things, how to enjoy
his enemies, how to avoid friendships. If he's unlucky
he will learn how to love and give everything away,
and how eventually he'll end up with nothing.

        Between himself and the grave his parents stand,
                monuments that will crumble.

        He won't understand many things.
He'll just accept them. He'll experiment with hardboiled
                eggs all his life
and die a stranger in a race attempting Humanity.

        And finally,
the playground full of dust,
        crates of sour milk lining the corridors;
                the headmaster, weeping quietly among the saws and
                                                                chisels

        in the damp woodwork room;

        The ghosts of Tim and Maureen and Patrick
        and Nancy and so many others,
        all confused with sexual longings, all
                doomed to living, and

one pale boy in a steamy room
looking out across the roofs and chimneys
where it seems the clouds are crying,
where ambitions are marked 'perishable',
where daylight's gone blind
and his teachers, all dead.

Without knowing much about it

ONE EVENING when the streams ran loudly
I went into a wood with two friends
Whose differences and arguments were genuine.
I had no idea what it was they were hunting.
One shouted out that the trees were glowing;
The other disagreed, insisting
The world was dull yet.

Between their arguments I wandered saying nothing;
In my head some minor pain was growing.
Aware now of the contradictions
All blood inherits,
Of the forces that through us were moving,
Fifteen and uncertain
I was smacked awake by loving.

Standing in invisible fire
I do not know what it was
That set our heads alight, or why—
Adventurous children,
What did we hope to find,
Not long before all directions vanished
And the leaves, glowing with both frost and sunlight,
Fell blindly about us?

Sleep now

In Memory of Wilfred Owen

SLEEP NOW,
Your blood moving in the quiet wind;
No longer afraid of the rabbits
Hurrying through the tall grass
Or the faces laughing from
The beach and among cold trees.

Sleep now,
Alone in the sleeves of grief,
Listening to clothes falling
And your flesh touching God;
To the chatter and backslapping
Of Christ meeting heroes of war.

Sleep now,
Your words have passed
The lights shining from the East
And the sound of flak
Raping graves and emptying seasons.

You do not hear the dry wind pray
Or the children play a game called soldiers
In the street.

Room

ROOM YOU'RE toneless now.
Room you don't belong to me
I want another room I want one
without your tatty memories
I want to brush you out into the streets where
you'll become a debris full of children's laughter
Room you're murderous
You make me feel like an accident
Make me blush with your crude jokes
and your old iron bedsteads
Room you've made me weep too many times
I'm sick of you and all your faces
I go into houses and find it's still you only this time
you're wearing a different disguise
I send out my spies to find you
They don't return
I send myself out and find you eating my spies.
It's impossible. You stand there dusty and naked
Your records spinning mutely
Your bed throwing gleaming girlbodies at the armies
of wage clerks who prance in you
Your books all empty
Your gas stoves hissing
Wallpaper crying sighing it doesn't matter
for your windows have become tape-recordings of the night
and only death will shove you to sleep.

I'm going to leave you
Going to spend all my dreams
Once in you I could lie and hear the spying moon apologise
as it tiptoed through the clouds
and left you in your special darkness.
But it's different now, now
only the rain splatters through
and the only other sound is you whispering
I'm not around you I'm in you all my walls are in you
Room you're full of my own graves!

Come into the city Maud

'Come into the garden, Maud,
  For the black bat, night, has flown.'
                        —Tennyson

MAUD, where are you Maud?
With your long dresses and peachcream complexion;
In what cage did you hang that black bat night?
What took place in the garden? Maud, it is over,
You can tell us now.

Still lyrical but much used, you wander about the suburbs
Watching the buses go past full of young happy people,
Wondering where the garden is, wherever can it be,
And how can it be lost. Maud, it's no use.

Can it be that you got yourself lost
And are living with an out of work musician,
You share a furnished room and have an old wireless
That tells you the latest bad news.
What's happening Maud?

Do you wear a Mary Quant dress
And eat fish and chips alone at night?
Wear make-up that tastes of forget-me-nots?
Where are you? and are you very lost,
Very much alone? Do you have stupendous dreams
And wake with one hand on your breast, and
The other on your cunt?
Do you cry for that garden, lost among pornographic
   suggestions,
Where the concrete flowers neither open nor close;
Who poured weedkiller over your innocence?

Maud, it's much later now.
Between the concrete banks the rivers of the sky run,
Black estuaries polluted by stars.
And daily beneath them
We wound ourselves,
Ignorant of any tenderness we hide in each other's lives
A clue to our loneliness.

We could not find that garden for you,
Even if we tried.
So, come into the city Maud,
Where flowers are too quickly picked
And the days are butchered as if they were enemies.

Maud, is that you I see
Alone among the office blocks,
Head bowed, young tears singing pop-sorrow
On your cheeks?

After breakfast

AFTER BREAKFAST,
Which is usually coffee and a view
Of teeming rain and the Cathedral old and grey but
Smelling good with grass and ferns
I go out thinking of all those people who've come into this room
And have slept here
Sad and naked
Alone in pairs
Who came together and
Were they young and white with
Some hint of innocence
Or did they come simply to come, to
Fumble then finally tumble apart;
Or were they older still, past sex,
Lost in mirrors, contemplating their decay and
What did the morning mean to them?

Perhaps once this room was the servant's quarters.
Was she young with freckles, with apple breasts?
Did she ever laugh?
Tease the manservant with her 19th Century charms
And her skirts whirling,
Did she look out through the skylight
And wish she were free, and
What did she have for breakfast?

Waking this morning I think
How good it would be
To have someone to share breakfast with.
Whole families waking!
A thousand negligées, pyjamas, nightgowns
All wandering warm down to breakfast
How secure!
And others coming out the far end of dawn
Having only drizzle and pain for breakfast,
Waking always to be greeted with the poor feast of daylight.

How many half-lives
Sulking behind these windows
From basement to attic
Complaining and asking
Who will inherit me today?
Who will I share breakfast with?
And always the same answer coming back—

The rain will inherit you—lonely breakfaster!

Prose poem towards a definition of itself

WHEN IN public poetry should take off its clothes and wave to the nearest person in sight; it should be seen in the company of thieves and lovers rather than that of journalists and publishers. On sighting mathematicians it should unhook the algebra from their minds and replace it with poetry; on sighting poets it should unhook poetry from their minds and replace it with algebra; it should fall in love with children and woo them with fairytales; it should wait on the landing for 2 years for its mates to come home then go outside and find them all dead.

When the electricity fails it should wear dark glasses and pretend to be blind. It should guide all those who are safe into the middle of busy roads and leave them there. It should shout EVIL! EVIL! from the roofs of the world's stock exchanges. It should not pretend to be a clerk or a librarian. It is the eventual sameness of contradictions. It should never weep until it is alone and then only after it has covered the mirrors and sealed up the cracks.

Poetry should seek out couples and wander with them into stables, neglected bedrooms and engineless cars for a final Good Time. It should enter burning factories too late to save anyone. It should pay no attention to its real name.

Poetry should be seen lying by the side of road accidents, be heard hissing from unlit gasrings. It should scrawl the teacher's secret on a blackboard, offer her a worm saying, Inside this is a tiny apple. Poetry should play hopscotch in the 6pm streets and look for jinks in other people's dustbins. At dawn it should leave the bedroom and catch the first bus home. It should be seen standing on the ledge of a skyscraper, on a bridge with a brick tied around its heart. It is the monster hiding in a child's dark room, it is the scar on a beautiful man's face. It is the last blade of grass being picked from the city park.

The beast

SOMETHING that was not there before
has come through the mirror
into my room.

It is not such a simple creature
as first I thought—
from somewhere it has brought a mischief

that troubles both silence and objects,
and now left alone here
I weave intricate reasons for its arrival.

They disintegrate. Today, in January, with
the light frozen on my window, I hear outside
a million panicking birds, and know even out there

comfort is done with; it has shattered
even the stars, this creature
at last come home to me.

A talk with a wood

MOVING THROUGH you one evening
when you offered shelter to
quiet things soaked in rain

I saw through your thinning branches
the beginnings of suburbs, and
frightened by the rain,

grey hares running upright in
distant fields, and quite alone there
thought of nothing but my footprints

being filled, and love, distilled
of people, drifted free, and then
the wood spoke to me.

The projectionist's nightmare

THIS IS the projectionist's nightmare:
A bird finds its way into the cinema,
finds the beam, flies down it,
smashes into a screen depicting a garden,
a sunset and two people being nice to each other.
Real blood, real intestines, slither down
the likeness of a tree.
'This is no good,' screams the audience,
'This is not what we came to see.'

Sad Adam

SAD ADAM
Uncurling from a concrete wall
Woken at dawn by rain and sudden light
You will move out now
Watching how the trees retreat down avenues of themselves
In your concrete century
Holding some vague idea of the sight you saw
When your eyes first clicked open into paradise

Here it seems
Even the stars are temporary
And the lives that spin beneath them
Rotate without memory.
Of the waiting world.
New Adam
In the markets touching apples
Huge exploding seeds!
Pink mirrors of the barrows!
You come in the brain
when market women offer you warm flowers

Or in rainpark cafés
Your teacup full of leaves
Escaping onto the open lawns
Afraid of the chained pathways
The green notice boards warning against sunset
Sorry for the frightened intruders
The winos and mad dawners escaped from cities
Who pin notes to their bodies then disappear.

Eveless Adam, touching yourself through blue shirts;
Your pale face reflecting in the rain
As the wind blows it passed and shatters it against leaves—
Twenty centuries are nothing here
The sickest headlines disintegrate
The selfish public world is cancelled out.

Yet for all your huge garden
From your own sad body
You cannot escape—
Let it make its own way out then,
Out across parks
And back into cities.
You'll return there coughing up bricks of dust,
Yet from that island you call a soul
Still slow birds will fly out and be evidence,
And on the walls of city banks
The memory of a leaf will sing.

The prophet's good idea

A NEW PROPHET appeared recently. He was first seen
walking out of an ocean. Which ocean?
It is so long ago we have forgotten.
But no other prophet suited so exactly
The spiritual climate.
                   He said
to the hushed crowds that had gathered,
to the journalists, the radio and television newscaster,
the anxious politicians:
                   'Stay in bed.'
That was his message. 'Bring each other
cups of lukewarm coffee,
lie naked as near as possible without touching,
think of governments, chewing-gum, ping-pong balls,
wars, Queen Elizabeth coronation cups, anything—
you're bound finally to burst out laughing.
Climb into bed. Imagine if everyone did.
Returning astronauts would hear
only the sound of souls snoring.'
      Well the hushed crowds, the journalists,
the radio and television newscasters,
the anxious politicians,
thought it sounded a good message, a clear message,
the kind they could pass on
quite harmlessly to children.
      Bed manufacturers were informed.
They loved the idea. Loved it. Made beds big enough
to hold several thousand people
all thinking of chewing-gum, ping-pong balls,
Queen Elizabeth coronation cups, anything—
      'It sounds so good a message,' said the people,
'that someting's bound to be wrong . . .'

So philosophers, scientists and a TV personality
gathered to discuss the message.
There were a few problems to be sorted out.
Robots were to be invented for the menial task
of running the planet. Otherwise, a fine message.
     And so now the whole planet's sleeping.
East and West snores, Hansel and Gretel personified.
Moss and moonwort burst out from bank-vaults,
all manner of creatures make themselves at home in houses.
From bed to bed spiders spin their webs, dream-catchers.
And there are sleep-walkers and sleep-lovers
and children born in sleep,
all wandering through fields and suburbs, all so quietly.
And some, woken into nightmare, comfort one another
whispering, '*Oh it's all madness.*'
               And occasionally the prophet,
to alleviate his immense boredom, rises from his ocean.
Occasionally he drags himself up into disused radio-ships
where, earphones to his brain, he listens,
makes sure it's all still silent.
And oh it's all madness, and he has little else to do,
him suffering in insomnia,
adrift in his fairy-tale silence.

Through the tall grass in your head

THROUGH THE TALL grass in your head
a grasshopper made out of stars is leaping;
It moves through those planets of information
Then leaves them behind it.
They'll soon explode.

You no longer bother watching how
Time and age leak down your mirror disfiguring it,
Nor how that animal the centuries have tamed
Roams less restless now inside you.

You have reached that state
Where so much has ceased to matter
And outside your window you see that the garden too
Has grown weary of sunlight,
And time has whittled down the cabbage leaves to thin white
    wings;
When memory, befuddled, drifted from your blood
All you did finally
Was to ask whether it was good.

Having taken the necessary precautions

HAVING TAKEN the necessary precautions against
honesty we were allowed to lie together,
messing up each others lives till mixing
the mess became intolerable. And then my love (if
I humorously might call you that) it was
the finger in the mouth or the stomach pump. Being
too polite to jump from buildings, fearing
the caretaker's wrath would reach heaven
and haunt us still further, pills sufficed.

We never quite managed to kill each other though
some strange attempts were made;
well practised in infidelities
even the most tender ones, their tongues red
lizards on spines, while together were suffocating
one less visible than themselves. Even those who
made gentleness a profession or art had something
about them that cancelled beauty. Anonymously we
sent warnings to ourselves, anonymously
we rejected each of them.

Flowers couldn't cover the hurts, the half-inch deaths
we piled up; a rose the size of two fists
wouldn't cover a pinprick of hating. Dreams larger
than ourselves we killed, not wanting
our smallness measured against them. Like greenfly
between the half-folded petals of a world we,
sleeping near its centre, blind to its colours,
nibble the heart out of it, till bloated
we lay dreamless, mind-blown in its ruins.

The song

BIRD SONG travels through gardens and reaches me.
For no particular reason I scoop up the song.
Once I would have sent it you
buried somewhere in cities
where fame and obscurity matter,
where dreams turn sour at breakfast.
But knowing I can do nothing but repeat
those truths we ourselves have made unworkable
I open my hand,
let the song free again.
Your ears might find it, your eyes trap its source
between garden and walls.
Presumptuous to offer as unique those things
we own in common; yet how common the heart
that without touching or wishing to own it,
lets the song nest there.

Portrait of a young girl raped at a suburban party

AND AFTER this quick bash in the dark
You will rise and go
Thinking of how empty you have grown
And of whether all the evening's care in front of mirrors
And the younger boys disowned
Led simply to this.

Confined to what you are expected to be
By what you are,
Out in this frozen garden
You shiver and vomit—
Frightened, drunk among trees,
You wonder at how those acts that called for tenderness
Were far from tender.

Now you have left your titterings about love
And your childishness behind you
Yet still far from being old
You spew up among flowers
And in the warm stale rooms
The party continues.

It seems you saw some use in moving away
from that group of drunken lives
Yet already ten minutes pregnant
In twenty thousand you might remember
This party
This dull Saturday evening
When planets rolled out of your eyes
And splashed down in suburban gardens.

Note to the hurrying man

ALL DAY I sit here doing nothing but
watching how at daybreak
birds fly out and return no fatter
when it's over. Yet hurrying about this room
you would have me do something similar;
would have me make myself a place
in that sad traffic you call a world.
    Don't hurry me into it; offer
no excuses, no apologies.
Until their brains snap open
I have no love for those who rush
about its mad business;
put their children on a starting line and push
into Christ knows what madness.

    You will not listen.
'Work at life!' you scream,
and working I see you rushing everywhere,
so fast most times you ignore
two quarters of your half a world.
    If all slow things are useless,
take no active part in nor justify your ignorance
that's fine; but why bother screaming after me?
Afraid perhaps to come to where I've stopped
in case you find
into some slow and glowing countryside
    yourself escaping.
Screams measure and keep up the distance between us:
    Be quieter—
I really do need to escape;
map out the route you might take
if ever this hurrying is over.

Note while walking home

WALKING HOME late, watched by all manner of things but
by nothing human; tree bark's glowing,
almost rain falling. My friends all in cities,
in Liverpool, in London, phoning
maybe loving, perhaps
wondering what to do this evening.
Rain that's not reached me yet
might fall on their roofs now,
mist up the bus windows behind which they are dreaming.
Here I wonder at how lives so invisible link,
touched by a common weather,
at how in the gap time makes between
hello and loneliness
memory teems; drenches.
Wandering home late
what I know of each separate person melts,
forms feelings I can express no better than
the wind that moves across me can.

Genesis

WITHOUT MUCH effort the piece of earth I was sitting on
broke off like fruit-cake from the ground
and drifted out of what we call the world.
Fortunately I had my winter clothes on,
for with every star I pass I'm growing colder.
It's a wondrous and amazing sight to see them pass
like bubbles in clear water.

I did not set out on this journey alone;
there were some picnickers here but they seemed
to shrink and disappear. Funny, they were
quite like myself at first.

Still there are some creatures left,
rabbits, squirrels, a few gibbering hares,
we join in a circle to keep warm
and as each fails and dies I take their fur
and bury myself beneath it.

If you see my shadow drift across your lawn,
the shadow of a man in winter clothes
sitting on a lump of soil,
you're bound to be amazed, but do not phone
an ambulance or the fire-brigade;
even helicopters could not reach me,
and spaceships I fear are too expensive.

Now I've grown used to it and as I said
with every star I pass I'm growing colder;
it's funny how new worlds are made and how
some pass through chaos to laughter.

School note

IN THE DORMITORIES the well-bred meat
is tucked away.
Safely for the evening
the rich little balls of meat
are tucked away.

Outside in the drive-way
the master's Rolls also sleeps,
a fat beetle among the trees,
shiny and silent it sleeps.

In the dormitories the well-bred meat
moves from the blankets.
Delighted to be left alone,
in hushed voices it chatters,
excited by the darkness.

You can hear the meat rustle out of its nightwear.
Tiptoeing round the beds,
the quiet meat playing.

Some portions, disdainful
of the giggles and the daring,
listen, deep into invention.

On itself the meat will practise daring games.
The lanky meat, the coy meat,
the round and innocent meat,
curious to discover
why it is so excitable.

Seen through the trees behind which you're walking

SEEN THROUGH the trees behind which you're walking
that girl, soaking and pale,
and the boy running her to shelter
near where the suburbs fade.

Let them find there a makeshift bed
where they can lie and listen
to the thin rain teeming and city droning
near to where they've hidden.

She'll be young and he not much older,
their bodies come alive,
their time there will stand against
the closing down of dreams.

And both lying, drenched, dishevelled
in a time when their world's shrunk, gone stale,
they'll sense their loving on such days
open it a while.

For in some obscene future moment
something in them will have shrivelled
choked by the ignorant mind
that gives love a local duty.

Let them lie down together
and not with another's guilt,
let them touch as the rain touches
the world and all its shapes.

For as his hands rest now wet against her
so they'll rest in time
against the memory of a shelter
where they stopped once in the rain.

Mr Jones takes over

LOOK, the Jones have moved into Paradise!
They've built a house there,
laid down a road or two,
built several yachts for the garden,
two garages, one church with its plastic vicar.

I asked hopefully when the lease would expire.
'We've bought the freehold,' they smiled.

The telephonists

The Engineer's Dream

H<small>E DREAMS</small>
Of the secret ways they would use him,
Of the worried gardens, the old ruins where they would take him
The pale girls
who never blush at the jokes he tells them
He dreams
For how can he imagine them anything other than beautiful
The young telephonists
Tuned into cities
Whose bodies receive and send out messages
Who travel down the warm long wires
To where something tender is being said

How difficult not to answer
The whispering voices
The hurried confessions
The first sentence broke at its centre
The last question left unanswered
How difficult to imagine
The girl three months pregnant
Who stumbling out her coded message
Breaks down, asks
Can you exterminate a generation?
And how with one quick call
Dreams can be aborted
And birds dozing on the wires tainted—
Through silence only the good messages go unheard
Stopping though the wires continue—

How can he imagine them
Anything other than beautiful
Those girls
Whose heads are jammed with the city's secrets
And yet how can he imagine
Their own bodies' failures
Or how easily they are lost and
The long wires sing
Of their own situations.

The lyric bird

AND THE lyric bird vomiting into blue air
falls back, its body shivering, wings broken.
Soon the sun will dry it out, insects gather.

Where did I first meet the lyric bird?
I met it at a skylight window or
in a garden among rusting pram wheels,
I met it soft beneath your dress.
Taking its shape from the earth's scents
I met the lyric bird in my head.

I sang with it for some time
and the lives around me
the sad lives
the brilliant lives
I ignored them.
I sang with the lyric bird.
It did not occur to me such birds can be amusing—
I was so glum!
It did not occur to me
its song might be
an echo of my own.

So I have taken the lyric bird and have examined it.
Said to it,
Go to that woman, blind among roses,
sing to her of their sweetness.
It obeyed me. It sang.

But the woman, something other than flowers obsessed her.
Go through her veins then,
fly up, up into the brain.
Sing to her
to remove her most common problem.
The bird remained silent.

And the lyric bird vomiting into blue air
falls back, its body shivering, wings broken.
Soon the sun will dry it out, insects gather.

The pint-sized Ark

WILLIAM STOOD in the encroaching dark
    Banging nails into a pint-sized Ark.
People gathered round and they mocked
Each single nail mad William knocked
Into the Ark, the pint-sized Ark,
Standing in the encroaching dark
Between the tower-blocks and the park.

William, banging, what's it for?
Don't you know it's been done before?

A policeman came, and he made a note:
'It's hardly the size of a rowing-boat.
The Ark's so small he will hardly get
Himself in along with the family pet.'

True, thought William, but my soul will fit,
And that's all need go into it.

BANG BANG drip BANG BANG drip
BANG drip BANG BANG drip BANG drip

His face was vacant, in his eye was a spark,
And his hammer beat in time to the encroaching dark.

You'd better believe him

A Fable

DISCOVERED an old rocking-horse in Woolworth's,
He tried to feed it, but without much luck.
So he stroked it, had a long conversation about
The trees it came from, the attics it had visited.
Tried to take it out then
But the store detective he
Called the store manager who
Called the police who in court next morning said,
'He acted strangely when arrested,
His statement read simply "I believe in rocking-horses".
We have reason to believe him mad.'
'Quite so,' said the prosecution,
'Bring in the rocking horse as evidence.'
'I'm afraid it escaped sir,' said the store manager,
'Left a hoof-print as evidence
On the skull of the store detective.'
'Quite so,' said the prosecution, fearful
of the neighing
Out in the corridor.

Old crock

I AM the very last astronaut, listen:
I send back messages from obscure planets;
smoke rises from the burning leaves,
something goes liquid beyond my reach.

I am the very last astronaut, listen:
I came here, surfacing like a whale
through oceans alchemists made real.

Listen: space-bugs scrape around the cockpit,
terror leaks in, spilling about the controls;
lice block the air tubes, eat into my brain.

I have forgotten my space pills, I
might explode.

About the brain: most is machinery anyway.
No worry there; only the memory now
feels soft and edible.

My only fear: that the lice might nest there,
eat out the shapes I've carried with me.
Still, I sense my loneliness breaking.

Someone else has arrived here,
space-jaunted naked, sits invisible here.
I'm obsolete, he tells me, holds up a mirror.

I am the very last astronaut, listen:
skull-white I grin,
skull-white and obviously mad.

Outside there are children playing
as if this blackness were a park,
dancing, their songs numerical—

I am too many centuries old.

In the brain-pan bits of machinery float,
still active, trying to get out the holes
where my eyes have been.

Ode on celestial music

(or: It's The Girl In The Bathroom Singing)

IT'S NOT celestial music it's the girl in the bathroom singing.
You can tell. Although it's winter
the trees outside her window have grown leaves,
all manner of flowers push up through the floorboards.
I think—what a filthy trick that is to play on me,
I snip them with my scissors shouting
'I want only bona fide celestial music!'
Hearing this she stops singing.

Out of her bath now the girl knocks on my door,
'Is my singing disturbing you?' she smiles entering,
'did you say it was licentious or sensual?
And excuse me, my bath towel's slipping.'
A warm and blonde creature
I slam the door on her breasts shouting
'I want only bona fide celestial music!'

Much later on in life I wear my hearing-aid.
What have I done to my body, ignoring it,
splitting things into so many pieces my hands
cannot mend anything? The stars, the buggers, remained silent.
Down in the bathroom now her daughter is singing.
Turning my hearing-aid full volume
I bend close to the floorboards hoping
for at least one song to get through.

The necessary slaughter

THERE WAS a bird come recently. When I went into my room
I saw it balanced on the open window.
It was a thin bird, I dreamt worms for it
And in the morning it was fatter.
And the next night for the worms
I dreamt rich soil, and then other creatures,
those that could not fly but now had ground on which to walk
all came and waited round my bed.
I dreamt for them what they needed,
the bird the worm, the fox, the hen, etc., etc.
right up to the two-legged creature.
Sadly the more they came the more
I had to dream for them each other's murder
Till my dreams became a planet and that planet called
The necessary slaughter.

The irrelevant song

A Pantomime of Kinds

WILLIAM wrote love songs.
In cafés, in ballrooms,
On seaside proms before the people had risen.
He translated all that the birds said.
He made his home in forests;
With a twig and ink from mushrooms
He would write on leaves,
On bark cut from tree-trunks.
He was your lover, was mine;
Was her lover, and his lover;
The total lover was William.
His songs, lyrical and splendid, became rivers.

Yet however early he had risen
The space beside him
Would be left vacant.
No shy ladies hurried down his morning pathway.
No small winter heel-prints dug into the soft ice.

Inside him most mornings frosty light gathered,
His loss grew branches,
Across his tongue
The world's tastes skated.

William, lost in downpours,
Dreamt in forests
Of simple, scented, singing
And repetitive bodies.
They pushed through the bushes to where he sat.
Hunched in the damp tree-roots,
Loose memory swilled about him.

William dreamt of bodies.
Mostly of long bodies.
The spines fur covered.
The skin by touch tightened.
Swan-like, lazy.

He wrote often of small breasted ladies met in village stations,
Of their healthy red noses,
Their legs in cord trousers.

He wrote of things that brought tears to the eyes of sparrows.
Even the crows built their nests low down
That they might listen.
Puffins worked their way inland through obscure rivers.
The sea had told them of William.
They listened from the damp bushes.
He wrote many love songs . . .
On trains going nowhere,
On the flyleafs of bibles.

In the animal and bird world he became famous.
Whales deep in oceans held literary conversations.
William, they said, was the great Human Lover.
O true mammal,
King of the Cloudy Kingdom,
O Poet Of The Multitude That Never Listens.

He wears a lion's mane in bed.
Wakes in golden fur.

William worked hard against his senses closing.
The belief that his touch was everlasting,
That cheeks, cool and loaded with scent, silence and days
   glowing
Would always stay turned towards him
Had not left him.
In such belief his light was founded.

Idiotic William
Passed 'teens
Passed twenties
Pruned his heart.

And so a story changes . . .

One morning he was visited by the Daughter of Sorrow.
Her name was Sympathy Unbuttoned.
Her eyes were green as meadows.
Small spiders nested in her curls.
Her breasts were non-existent.

They wandered together
Daily,
Weekly,
Wandered in woodland making new pathways.

Where the trees thinned out,
Where the deep rivers shallowed,
They found estuaries,
Mudflats,
Herring-gulls,
The awkward sandpipers,
The small boats stranded in which
None drowned ever.

Thin William spoke his verses;
His lady listened.
Breathless and breastless
She listened in wonder.

When in winter his tongue was frozen
And on his cheeks
Rain also had frozen
She watched his village girls,
His proms,
His ballroom and cafés
Pass in icy procession from eyelid to cheek-bone.

For her he tried to protect the rivers.
They went underground.
Lost in bramble and cool stone darkness
They escaped him.

He asked the birds for more song,
More variety.
More! More!
Their throats dried up.
Now all day they sleep in their branches.

Why are the fields barren?
For her William has gathered in the flowers,
Frightened else the evening freezes them.

The cottage is in darkness.
He has closed the shutters else
Hailstones smash the windows.

His lady is pleased.

Good morning William,
On your way into light
How can you fail to notice
The blackbirds frozen in their nests,
Or how eternity is littered
With irrelevant deaths?

Didn't the larks warn you
That nothing is for ever?
That in the stoat's den the rabbit leaves no message?

Didn't the tree's branches warn you
Blown leaves don't mind parting?
The sad endings you pursue
Are but things completed,

The yawning hares in a landscape of heather
Do not wonder if they will outlive one another
Nor why the scented winds
Splash down among them.

William wrote long songs . . .
But the birds in the woodland,
The whales in the oceans,
The puffins and sparrows
And awkward sandpipers
Lost faith.

His first songs,
The loneliest,
The loveliest,
Fled into an irretrievable country.

In the Daughter of Sadness
Breastless in forests,
All his songs had gathered.

In so single a lady
No great dream could be founded;
Among the curls and the spiders
His eyes had rested.

The songs grew dreamless,
The pathways clotted,
A memory of light leapt about in the forests,
And the Daughter of Sadness
Ironed out his shadows
For William to wear
On his way through the seasons.

And so with this a story's ending.
William woke. He rose from out
His own love sick shadow.

When field, lake, river, mist and valley
Closed down its wonder,
In a peculiar season
Caught between dyings,
William disowned her.
From his sight then the blurred lights drifted.
What was left was yet to be encountered.

Rain drowned the valleys;
In a catacomb of soaking grass
Grounded birds were crying.
His dark was internal but soon
It stepped outwards.
Into his songs there leaked
More awkward celebrations;
Messages sent via lark and rose
Relinquished any meaning.

William wrote love songs,
Where the thin grasses had perished,
Where the night hugged its own shapes
And love hugged its habits.

Interruption at the opera house

AT THE very beginning of an important symphony,
while the rich and famous were settling into their quietly
expensive boxes,

a man came crashing through the crowds,
carrying in his hand a cage in which
the rightful owner of the music sat,
yellow and tiny and very poor;
and taking onto the rostrum this rather timid bird
he turned up the microphones, and it sang.

'A very original beginning to the evening,' said the crowds,
quietly glancing at their programmes to find
the significance of the intrusion.

Meanwhile at the box office, the organizers of the evening
were arranging for small and uniformed attendants
to evict, even forcefully, the intruders.
But as the attendants, poor and gathered from the nearby
slums at little expense,
went rushing down the aisles to do their job
they heard, above the coughing and irritable rattle of jewels,
a sound that filled their heads with light,
and from somewhere inside them there bubbled up a stream,
and there came a breeze on which their youth was carried.
How sweetly the bird sang!

And though soon the fur-wrapped crowds
were leaving their boxes and in confusion were winding their
way home
still the attendants sat in the aisles,
and some, so delighted at what they heard, rushed out to call
their families and friends.

And their children came,
sleepy for it was late in the evening,
very late in the evening,
and they hardly knew if they had done with dreaming
or had begun again.

In all the tenement blocks
the lights were clicking on,
and the rightful owner of the music,
tiny and no longer timid, sang
for the rightful owners of the song.

Spring song

I THOUGHT the tree was rather ordinary until yesterday
when seven girls in orange swim-wear climbed into its
branches.
Laughing and giggling they unstrapped each other,
letting their breasts fall out,
running fourteen nipples along the branches.
I sat at my window watching.
'Hey,' I said, 'what are yous doing up there?'
'We are coaxing out the small green buds earlier than usual,'
said the first.
Then the second slid down the tree—amazing how brown her
                                                    body was—
and naked she lay on the dead clumpy soil for an hour or more.
On rising there was a brilliant green shape of grass
and the beginning of daisies.

'Are you Spring?' I asked.
'Yes,' she replied. 'And the others also, they are Spring.'
I should have guessed.
What other season permits such nakedness?

The others came in through the window then.
All the dust the room had gathered vanished.
They are the happy gardeners;
their long backs bend to gather cartloads of sadness
and take it elsewhere.

They'll walk among us making our touch perfect.
Their beauty more awkward than even the topmost models,
they'll take our hearts to the laundry
and there'll be but joy in whatever rooms we wake.
We'll love all in that country
where couples glow brilliant
and the craziest amongst them find in their bodies
a promise of laughter.

Cosmic misery

IN THE MORNING I get up and there is nothing to do
I tell myself it is only temporary

In the afternoons I am bored I dislike what I am
I tell myself it is only temporary

In the evening I meet a woman I no longer care for
I tell myself it is only temporary

At night alone confused I listen to my heart beating
I tell myself it is only te

The unicorn

SHE'S PULLED down the blinds now, she's locking the door,
a unicorn's just stepped down from the wall;
naked as snow on the eiderdown
it's rested its head and its horn.

She's pulled down the blinds now, it's warmer inside,
naked she crosses the room;
the eiderdown's blue and her hair is blonde
and white is the unicorn.

Dreaming, though both far from sleep,
both head and body spin around,
and humming deep into her veins
moves now the unicorn.

Frightened once by normal flesh
her body disallowed
ordinary shapes to entertain her,
even buried deep in dreams—

for touched too soon in hurrying rooms,
the walls, forests they became,
and into myth she faded,
leaf-eyed; birds sang inside her brain.

She's pulled down the blinds now, she's locked the door,
fists bunched tight against a wall;
the eiderdown's blue and her hair is blonde
and red now the unicorn.

Albatross ramble

I WOKE this morning to find an albatross staring at me.
Funny, it wasn't there last night.
Last night I was alone.

The albatross lay on the bed.
The sheets were soaking.

I live miles from any coast.
I invited no mad sailors home.
I dreamt of no oceans.

The bird is alive, it watches me carefully.
I watch it carefully.
For some particular reason I think
Maybe we deserve one another.

It's sunny outside, spring even.
The sky is bright; it is alive.

I remember I have someone to meet,
Someone clear, someone with whom I'm calm,
Someone who lets things glow.

As I put on my overcoat to go out
I think that maybe after all
I don't deserve this bird.

Albatrosses cause hang-ups.
There's not much I can do with them.
I can't give them in to zoos.
The attendants have enough albatrosses.

Nobody is particularly eager to take it from me.

I think, Maybe, the bird's in the wrong house.
Maybe it meant to go next door.
Maybe some sailor lives next door.
Maybe it belongs to the man upstairs.
Maybe it belongs to the girls in the basement.
It must belong to someone.

I rush into the corridor and shout:
'Does anyone own an albatross? Has anyone lost it?
There's an albatross in my room!'

I'm met by an awkward silence.

I know the man upstairs is not happy.
I know the girls in the basement wander lost among the
    furniture.
Maybe they're trying to get rid of it
And won't own up.
Maybe they've palmed the albatross off on me.

I don't want an albatross; I don't want this bird;
I've got someone to meet,
Someone patient, someone good and healthy,
Someone whose hands are warm and whose grin
Makes everything babble and say yes.
I'd not like my friend to meet the albatross.

It would eat those smiles;
It would bother that patience;
It would peck at those hands
Till they turned sour and ancient.

Although I have made albatross traps,
Although I have sprayed the thing with glue,
Although I have fed it every poison available,
It persists in living,
This bird with peculiar shadows
Cast its darkness over everything

If I go out it would only follow me.
It would flop in the seat next to me on the bus,
Scowling at the passengers.
If I took it to the park it would only bother the ducks,
Haunt couples in rowing boats,
Tell the trees it's winter.
It would be patted by policemen as they gently asked:
'Have you an albatross licence?'

Gloom bird, doom bird,
I can do nothing about it.
There are no albatross-exterminators in the directory;
I looked for hours.

Maybe it will stay with me right through summer;
Maybe it has no intentions of leaving.
I'll grow disturbed with this bird never leaving,
This alien bird with me all the time.

And now my friend is knocking on the door,
Less patient, frowning,
A bit sad and angry.

I'll sit behind this door and make noises like an albatross.
A terrible crying.
I'll put my mouth to the keyhole and wail albatross wails.
My friend will know then
I have an albatross in my room.
My friend will sympathize with me,
Go away knowing it's not my fault I can't open the door.

I'll wait here; I might devise some plan:
It's spring and everything is good but for this.
This morning I woke with an albatross in my room.
There's nothing much I can do about it until it goes away.

It's selfish to be happy, say the gloomy

IT MUST BE upsetting to be happy.
It must be embarrassing.
Specially now, specially around now,
It must be unnerving.

What can the happy say? How can
they not look ridiculous?
It's not a time for happiness, specially now,
specially around now, say the gloomy.

Who'd believe them anyway?
Who'd believe it if they said
numerous miracles are about to happen.
We live in a time without miracles.

Maybe that's why it's embarrassing.
In a smug time, in a time without astonishment,
in a time that's done away with wonder.
It must be unnerving.

It must be upsetting also to feel
much of passion, to move through a city,
awake, jubilant, to dance when
all about disasters are occurring.

How can you possibly remain happy,
How can you be so callous, so arrogant?
Specially now, specially around now?
It's selfish to be happy, say the gloomy.

The main character

T HE HERO
Thinks the hero is the main character,
The heroine
Thinks the heroine is the main character,
The audience is enthralled but
Has not much say in the matter.
For the main character is still out in the wings,
He has not yet appeared.
Appalling crimes are committed,
Appalling sorrows crawl across the stage and fall
Into the laps of the audience.
Ambitions are proven absurd,
Times are slaughtered,
Great speeches are made and revoked,
The stage is set for a Major Revelation and still
The main character sits in the wings,
Twiddling his thumbs.
For no one has told him exactly what it is he must do
To bring the play to a fruitful conclusion.
And so it goes on and on and on,
And appalling crimes are committed,
And great speeches are made and revoked,
And still the main character
(Who was specially chosen for the part)
Sits exhausted in the wings,
Twiddling his thumbs.

The literary gathering

IN THOSE rooms I became more distant than ever.
Where once I went with my head down,
Mumbling answers to obscure questions,
I felt a total stranger.

Poem-freak!
I felt I'd perverted imagination.
I had no real answers.
I'd left my brain at home preserved in lime.

Like a dumb canary let out of its cage
I'd found another cage.
It did not suit me.
In my beak the invitations melted.

Standing there I shook from sleep
What had into sleep escaped.
I glanced around the books for friends,
Found only mannequins dressed in the latest fashion.

Those for whom I sang were not there,
But were instead outside, and laughing drunk
Climbed railings in some public park,
Not caring where it was they went.

Outside again I was alive again.
I begged my soul to be anonymous, to breathe
Free of obscure ambitions and the need
To explain away any song.

The giant seen

A Riddle

I STRETCH beside the body of morning.
A lark's in my fist.
In the clear lake's bottom
My feet are resting.

My hair, blown outwards, is wrapped round clouds.
I do not stalk anything.
Centre-ways between ground and lightning
My stomach rumbles. My sight is not blocked by mountains.
I can gaze into the sun forever.

I bestow everything upon everything: land,
Oceans, air-streams and seasons,
The rest.
I don't know where I get it all from.

There is something in the background whispering
That has never stopped whispering,
Letting me be;
Under the camouflage of planets
It wags a tongue.

I stretch beside the body of morning,
The pressure that shapes a rose:
Solid, to the senses at least,
Tangible.
The valleys hung upside down
Wait now till I am recognized.

Travelling between places

LEAVING NOTHING and nothing ahead;
when you stop for the evening
the sky will be in ruins,

when you hear late birds
with tired throats singing
think how good it is that they,

knowing you were coming,
stayed up late to greet you
who travels between places

when the late afternoon
drifts into the woods, when
nothing matters specially.

The obsolete nightingale

(A continuation of Prosepoem towards a definition of
   itself)

WHEN LONG ago it became apparent that the lion
     had no intentions of lying down with the lamb
you, still believing in that obsolete fable,
were thrown into chaos.

From somewhere inside you
time and again you dragged out the lamb,
and inviting the lion in from the nervous world
put the fable to the test.

Each night through the walls the slaughter leaked,
your neighbours became addicted.

A terminal romantic, a confused source-seeker,
in the bedrooms of cheap hotels you open your suitcase,
and unfolding the soiled rainbows
sleep among them.

                                    *

Poetry is the interval during which nothing is said,
the sign-board on which nothing is written.
It is the astronaut stepping from the first time into liquid
     space
It follows its imagination out across the frozen lakes,
out to where the small footprints have ended.

It is the surgeon cutting deeper and deeper,
bewildered by the depths.
It sings for the children who keep clouds in their pockets,
for the midwives tasting of grass,
for the impending dust,
for the card-dealers who pull out the milky way
as a last resort.

At the festival of fools it erects a bedraggled maypole
and dances to a music of its own invention.

In the conference rooms where the great minds gather
where the politicians squark
and the philosophers brood
it serves the drinks,
in the halls where the fashionable dance
it robs the overcoats.

It stands in red kiosks exhausting
the phone books of generations.
It is the acceptable lie in a time
of acceptable lies.

*

When the professor of literature steps into the shadow of a
    lectern
and when the students are finally seated
and the whispers have died away
poetry puts on an overcoat
and sick of threadbare souls,
steps out into the streets weeping.

It is the clue overlooked by policemen;
the stranger walking through the airport terminal;
the blue egg found crushed in a nest.

It is the address thrown from the window
of a passing train.

*

I sit in motorway cafes staring through windows.
You are there,
running across the wet fields,
the logicians howling after you.

They have given the hounds platefuls of roses,
stuffed their noses with tulips—
they'll give you no rest, poetry.
From the roofs of articulate houses
the scholars will snipe at you.

It is rumoured one among them
has transmuted gold into dust.

I have found you among strangers,
among faces that pick about in time,
choosing the length of their days
and the length of their suffering.

*

I have found you most often in sadness,
on evenings when each patch of ground
seems remote as an island,
when rooms are bleakest and speech is incoherent,
when words choke,
fish thrown up from the paranoiac pools.

You belong to these generations drifting between buildings,
unlovely mammals, pale as worms,
lamenting their own temporariness.
You are the chameleon crawling across rainbows.

I am anchored among your contradictions:
Wrapped in obsolete kindness,
too caring in days ruled by slaughter,
too gentle among the truncheons and the nights fed on
    disaster
you wander about the city whispering
'Where's the bloodbath this evening?'
'What new mutilations are available?'
You wander through each face looking for the one
that will best mirror your own.
The list of your affairs is endless.

*

Poetry asks the head-office for its files on the nightingale,
for all information regarding its colour,
its shape, the kind of song it indulged in.
The message comes back:
'Subject obsolete. File closed.'

6.15 am
Across the Thames busloads of charladies wander
gossiping about disease;
truckloads of bleached meat unloaded in front of futuristic
   towers.
Worn faces, faded print dresses,
exhausted overcoats,
all refusing to announce the daylight as miracle.
Poetry, you were born among them.

The Embankment is thick with rain,
with cardboard boxes in which dignity flounders.
From the river poetry fishes out an image
of a dead bird floating beneath vanished starlight.

It is the same old story.
Night owns the copyright.

And always there will be the dream of travelling,
of boarding the boats sailing from trivia,
And always there will be the regret,
the sense of carnivals finished.

Poetry, what of your education? Early on you learned to loathe the
literati's clever games – those spiels for the intellect that left
untouched people stuck in the rut down which most human
longings flow. Your vocabulary was limited, you studied im-
possibilities, wrote essays on impatience that were never finished,
you stared at the atlas, invented journeys you were too young to set
out upon. You planned meetings with alien invaders. In the school
laboratories you invented a cure for obedience.

Were you hidden, disguised as frost on the spiky railings of schoolyards? Did you sneak into the classroom and settle, quiet as dust, onto the shoulders of restless children? Time and again I have gone to you for advice and searching through pages of unremarkable confessions have found among the heart's trash nothing but revelations. You are the mirror in front of which the years tremble. You are the laughter borrowed momentarily from strangers. You are the final sentence, echoing forever.

'If you had to hazard a guess who would you say your poetry is for?'

FOR PEOPLE who have nowhere to go in the afternoons,
For people who the evening banishes to small rooms,
For good people, people huge as the world.
For people who give themselves away forgetting
What it is they are giving,
And who are never reminded.
For people who cannot help being kind
To the hand bunched in pain against them.
For inarticulate people,
People who invent their own ugliness,
Who invent pain, terrified of blankness;
And for people who stand forever at the same junction
Waiting for the chances that have passed.
And for those who lie in ambush for themselves,
Who invent toughness as a kind of disguise,
Who, lost in their narrow and self-defeating worlds,
Carry remorse inside them like a plague;
And for the self-seeking self lost among them
I hazard a poem.

Nursery rhyme for the sleepless

'SUCKABLOOD, Suckablood, where have you been?'
'I've been in the brain of a Dreaming Machine.'

'Suckablood, Suckablood, what did you there ?'
'I taught it of sorrow and loss, pain and despair.'

'Suckablood, Suckablood, were the lessons much fun?'
'I spoke sombrely of all that is soon come and soon gone.

'Suckablood, Suckablood, does it know what you've done!?'
'I think it has some inkling of what has begun.'

'If it wants no more lessons, then what's to be done?'
'Don't worry, to me I am sure it will come.'

'Suckablood, Suckablood, what if it's late?'
'Then in the grave my lessons will keep.'

After frost

IT'S HARD to tell what bird it is
Singing in the misty wood,
Or the reason for its song
So late after evening's come.

When all else has dropped its name
Down into the scented dark
Its song grown cool and clear says
Nothing much to anyone,

But catches hold a whisper in my brain
That only now is understood.
It says, rest your life against this song,
It's rest enough for anyone.

Believing in the wall

BLUNDERING AGAIN,
I found myself in a strange neighbourhood.
I walked into a cul-de-sac at the end of which
A familiar wall was waiting.
Behind me was a mess, a maze of spiritual failures.

To put right again all that had gone wrong
Was a dream I did not care for.
I sat on a stone beside the wall.
Memories spawned, their secrets stung me.

To while away the time until some improbable event occurred
I took out my history and examined it.
On moss beside the stone I laid out my ambitions;
The awkward affairs, the imperfect insights.
To see them was a potion of kinds,
A way of understanding.

Beside the wall I made up fantasies.
I was sure all other streets led to neighbourhoods
From which all longings were banished,
Where at night in the bright halls
People danced like may-flies,
Where everything that ever ached had been replaced
By sensation too brief for pain.

Believing the wall real I sat beside it scheming.
Unintelligent dreamer, buffoon, I finally dreamed
A route through its bricks and found
A familiar wall was waiting.

Night piece

ALL DAY I have spent building this web,
This necessary extension strung between
Objects unfamiliar and uncertain.
Over those things to which it is anchored
I have no power. My trust must be explicit.
So far I have caught rain, sunlight,
Particles of leaf, and things so small
They cannot satisfy.
At night in a crack between concrete
I dream of catching something so immense
It would shake the web's centre;
Awkward and meat-ridden, its wings
Would snap and dullen my creation.
Of such an event I am terrified,
For such an event I am longing.

Winter note

IT'S EVENING and the streets are cold again.
The cars go past in such a hurry you'd think
The world full of emergencies.
The young men and women no longer parading
Hurry from the supermarkets,
Feigning a lack of caring, their tins
Glow with loneliness.
Leaves gone, scents gossip of previous winters.

And what did we do then?
Were the florists' windows stuffed with bright icy
    flowers?
Were the sirens as persistent, the parks as barren?
Whose hand was held, whose face
Did we swear never to forget?

As always the rooms are damp, the furniture ancient.
Yet among this drabness is a light, self-created.
The wine stains on the carpet emerge as roses,
The fridge becomes a grotto.
We fill our heads with dreams still.
In this season we are all that blossoms.

Hopeful

ALONE, tired, exhausted even
by what had not yet happened,
passing a cemetery on the outskirts of London I saw
an angel dip its hand into a grave
and pull out a fistful of cherry-blossom.

Waves

AND THE ONE throwing the lifebelt,
Even he needs help at times,
Stranded on the beach,
Terrified of the waves.

In the high-rise Alice dreams of Wonderland

SHE RECEIVED a parcel through the post.
It had everything she wanted inside it.
Sometimes when she touched it
A planet-sized man would come to the door
And say exactly the right kind of thing.
The parcel kept her happy,
Provided all she needed.
Her children blossomed,
Grew fat and pink and healthy.
The high-rise in which she lived shrank,
Became a neat house—
A swing on the lawn, a driveway, etc., etc., etc.
A bill for the parcel arrived on Monday.
On Tuesday came a reminder.
On Wednesday came a solicitor's letter.
On Thursday came a court order.
On Friday the jury gave a verdict.
On Saturday the parcel was taken.
Most days
Alice can be seen in the high-rise,
Mouth twisted, weeping.

Meat

SOME PRETTY little thoughts,
some wise little songs,
some neatly packed observations,
some descriptions of peacocks, of sunsets,
some fat little tears,
something to hold to chubby breasts,
something to put down,
something to sigh about,
I don't want to give you these things.
I want to give you meat,
the splendid meat,
the blemished meat.
Say, here it is,
here is the active ingredient,
the thing that bothers history,
that bothers priest and financier.
Here is the meat.

The sirens wailing on police-cars,
the ambulances alert with pain,
the bricks falling on the young
queens in night-parks
demand meat,
the real thing.

I want to give you something
that bleeds as it leaves my hand
and enters yours,
something that by its rawness,
that by its bleeding
demands to be called real.

In the morning, when you wake,
the sheets are blood-soaked.

For no apparent reason
they're soaked in blood.
Here is the evidence you have been waiting for.
Here is the minor relevation.

A fly made out of meat lands
on a wall made out of meat.
There is meat in the pillows we lie on.
The eiderdowns are full of meat.
I want to give it you,
share the headache of the doctor
bending irritated by the beds
as he deals out the hushed truth about the meat,
the meat that can't be saved,
that's got to end,
that's going to be tossed away.

At night the meat rocks between sheets
butchered by its longings.

You can strip the meat,
you can caress and have sex with it—
the thing that carries its pain around,
that's born in pain,
that lives in pain,
that eats itself to keep itself in pain.

My neighbours driving away in their cars
are moody and quiet and do not talk much.
I want to fill their cars with meat,
stuff it down their televisions,
I want to leave it in the laundromats
where the shy secretaries gather.

At the fashionable parties the fashionable meat dances,
studded with jewellery it dances.
How delicately it hold its wine glass,
How intelligently it discusses
the latest mass butchering.

Repetitive among the petals,
among the songs repetitive,
I want the stuff to breathe its name,
the artery to open up and whisper:

I am the meat,
the sole inventor of paradise.
I am the thing denied entrance into heaven,
awkward and perishable,
the most neglected of mammals.
I am the meat that glitters,
that weeps over its temporariness.

I want the furniture to turn into meat,
the door handle as you touch it
to change into meat.

The meat you are shy to take home to mother,
the meat you are,
gone fat and awkward.
Hang it above your bed.
In the morning when you wake drowsy
find it in the wash-basin.
Nail it to the front door.
In the evening leave it out on the lawns.
The meat that thinks the stars are white flies.
Let the dawn traveller find it among hedgrows
waiting to offer itself as he passes.
Leave it out among the night-patrols and the lovers.
Leave it between the memorandums of politicians.

Here is the active ingredient;
here is the thing that bothers history,
that bothers priest and financier.
Pimply and blunt and white,
It comes towards me with its arms outstretched.
I am in love with the meat.

The wrong number

ONE NIGHT I went through the telephone book name by
name.
   I moved in alphabetical order through London
Plundering living-rooms, basements, attics,
   Brothels and embassies.
I phoned florists' shops and mortuaries,
   Politicians and criminals with a flair for crime;
At midnight I phoned butchers and haunted them with strange
   bleatings.
I phoned prisons and zoos simultaneously,
I phoned eminent surgeons at exactly the wrong moment.
   Before I was half-way through the phone book
My finger was numb and bloody.
   Not satisfied with the answers I tried again.
Moving frantically from A to Z needing confirmation
   That I was not alone
I phoned grand arsonists who lived in the suburbs
   And rode bicycles made out of flames.
No doubt my calls disturbed people on their deathbeds,
   Their death rattles drowned by the constant ringing of
     telephones!
No doubt the various angels who stood beside them
   Thought me a complete nuisance.
I *was* a complete nuisance.
   I worried jealous husbands to distraction
And put various Casanovas off their stroke
   And woke couples drugged on love.

I kept the entire London telephone system busy,
    Darting from phone booth to phone booth
The Metropolitan phone-squad always one call behind me.
    I sallied forth dressed in loneliness and paranoia—
The Phantom Connection.
    Moving from shadow to shadow,
Rushing from phone booth to phone booth till finally
    I sought out a forgotten number and dialled it.
A voice crackling with despair answered.
    I recognized my own voice and had nothing to say to it.

I studied telephones constantly

SO I STUDIED telephones constantly.
I wrote great and learned papers on the meaning of
    telephones.
I wondered what the last dispatch rider thought
galloping past the telephone wires, his body full of stale
    arrows.
I wondered what it would have been like
If Caesar had had a telephone.

I thought of nothing but telephones.
Night after night I invented numbers.
I placed trunk-calls to non-existent cities.
Jesus! I received so many weird replies.

I wondered if the dead would like a telephone.
Perhaps we should plant phones in graves so that the dead
might hold endless conversations
gulping in the warm earth.

Telegrams and telephones,
and not an ounce of flesh between them
only so much pain.

I began to consider them my enemy.
I joined underground movements dedicated to their
    overthrowal.
I vowed absurd vows,
I sacrificed daisies.
My hands were bloody with pollen.

I can imagine the night when waking from a nervous sleep
you find the telephone has dragged itself up the stairs one

                                        at a time

and sits mewing,
the electronic pet waiting for its bowl of words.

            *

Hello! Hello!
It's the evening phone-in show!
You've an abscess on the heart?
A tumour on the soul?
You're sleepless with grief?
You're in pain, you feel insane?
Neglected? Rejected?
You feel like a freak,
You feel bleak?
Lost your wife last week?

You're alone? Dying on your own?
Cancer crawling up the spine?
Well, fine!
Don't worry, don't care.
I'm on the air!
I'm DJ Despair,
I reek of the right answers!

*

It is so far from the beginning of telephones.

I thought of how it felt to be connected for the first time,
to be fifteen and uncertain while her mother says: 'Hang on'.
O the ecstasy of waiting for her to come down from her young
　　　room and answer!
The pinkness of telephones and the fragrance of telephones
　　And the innocence and earnestness of telephones!
I'm sure those wires still cross paradise,
still fresh in the crushed ice of Yes!

Nothing in that conversation has changed.
She is still bemused at his agony as he struggles
　　　with the language of telephones.
O to be connected so!
Before shadows passed over the wires,
before trivia weighed them down,
when they trilled like sparrows and their voices were bright.

Where does God hide his telephone number?
No doubt the clergy have committed that number to memory.
Kneeling in their celestial phone booths
they phone him late at night while the lambs are suffering.
For the telephone is hard to resist
For it brings joy and misery without distinction
For the telephone is blameless
For it is a blessing to the hypochondriac
Both 'Help' and 'No' are in the word telephone.

And would it have made much difference
if Faustus had had a telephone?
Whose number was on Marilyn Monroe's lips the last time she
felt too tired?
What went wrong?
I was listening to the grave gossip.
Terror leaked from the mouth's pit.

In telephone exchanges the world over
The numbers are dying,
Vast morgues where the operators sleep-walk among the
babble,
Where the ghost phones lament
for all the calls that went wrong.

Death owns everyone's telephone number.

And the night?
How many telephone numbers does the night possess?
The night has as many telephone numbers as stars.

Turning the pages

LATE AT NIGHT I sat turning the pages,
Half-looking for the lines I'd once read,
Astonished at their simplicity.
Late at night I sat turning the pages,
My tongue uprooting miniature lights, infatuated
By what it hoped to become.
I sat turning the pages ignoring
The voices asking,
'What answers can be found
By simply turning the pages?'
While the future amassed its griefs
And things left undone squabbled and multiplied
I sat turning the pages,
And slowly I learned
How to abandon the future
And leave it less crowded,
And I began to understand
How there is nothing complicated in this world
That is not of my own making,
And how for years I had lived
Under the scrutiny of the blind,
Believing they could see me best.
Lacking confidence not in what I was
But in what others considered me
I almost became what they considered me.
And now I am glad I lacked such confidence,
And sat late at night turning the pages ignoring
The voices asking,
What answers can be found
By simply turning the pages,
Late at night turning the pages half-looking
For the lines you once read,
Astonished at their simplicity.

I tried to find my voice

I TRIED to find my voice, a voice lost
In a night thickened by paranoia,
In a night crowded out by doubts
It could not articulate.
I had let go of it through negligence,
As at a carnival one lets go a child's hand.

I rummaged through a jumble sale of bodies,
Listened to advice devoid of meaning;
My voice was like a moth, its few colours
Worn to exhaustion.
It was drunk and lost, it was battered
And flung everywhere.

I tried to find it in the beds
Of solemn girls disguised as women,
I tried to find it among the men I envied.
I searched for it among its own inventions.

I had arranged my life around that voice.
Absurdly relied on it to explain
Who and what I was, as if either mattered.
In strange towns I used it to advantage.
Whatever it could fish out from the night
I accepted.

No matter; it was the one voice I let delude me.
Maybe it was getting the better of me,
Maybe it was envious and screamed at times,
Certainly it said things of which I'd grown ashamed
But I forgave it its blindness and tantrums
Hoping it would change.

And now it is beyond change.
My mouth cannot find it.
I have lost it; and no longer wish it back.
In winter I will make a voice out of snow,
In spring I will make a voice out of flowers,
In summer and autumn I will make a voice
With what is at hand.

The complaints it carried like credentials are misplaced
And its mouthful of reasons are blown away,
And its mouthful of tragedies
Have become light as dandelion seeds.

Blake's purest daughter

'All things pass,
Love and mankind is grass'
—Stevie Smith

MUST SHE always walk with Death, must she?
I went out and asked the sky.
No, it said, no,
She'll do as I do, as I do.
I go on forever.

Must she always walk with Death, must she?
I went and asked the soil.
No, it said, no,
She'll do as I do, as I do.
I will nourish her forever.

Must she always walk with Death, must she?
I listened to the water.
No, it said, no.
She'll do as I do, as I do.
I will cleanse her forever.

Must she always walk with Death, must she?
No, said the fire,
She'll burn as I burn, as I burn.
She will be in brilliance forever.

O but I am not Death, said Death slyly,
I am only no longer living,
Only no longer knowing exorbitant grief.
Do not fear me, so many share me.

Stevie elemental
Free now of the personal,
Through sky and soil
And fire and water
Swim on, Blake's purest daughter!

Pipe dream

IF I COULD choose
The hour in which
Death chooses me,
And the way in which
It will make its arbitrary choice,
I can think of nothing better than
To fall asleep near midnight in a boat
As it enters a new port,
In a boat
With a clarity of stars above
And below it,
And all around me
Bright music and voices laughing in
A language not known to me.
I'd like to go that way,
Tired and glad,
With all my future before me,
Hungry still for the fat
And visible globe.

Drunk

An interpretation of Baudelaire's prose poem,
The Drunken Song

PEOPLE ARE sober as cemetery stones!
They should be drunk, we should all be drunk!
Look, it's nearly night time and the sober news
Comes dribbling out of television sets—
It should be drunken news,
If only it were drunken news!
Only festivals to report and the sombre death
Of one ancient daisy.

It's time to get drunk, surely it's time?
Little else matters;
Sober the years twist you up,
Sober the days crawl by ugly and hunched and your soul—
It becomes like a stick insect!

I've spent so much time in the company
Of sober and respectable men,
And I learned how each sober thought is an obstacle laid
Between us and paradise.
We need to wash their words away,
We need to be drunk, to dance in the certainty
That drunkenness is right.

So come on, let's get drunk,
Let's instigate something!
Let's get drunk on whatever we want—
On songs, on sex, on dancing,
On tulip juice or meditations,
It doesn't matter what—

But no soberness, not that!
It's obscene!
When everything you deluded yourself you wanted has gone
You can get drunk on the loss,
When you've rid yourself of the need for those things back
Then you will be light,
You will be truly drunk.

For everything not tied down is drunk—
Boats and balloons, aeroplanes and stars—
All drunk.
And the morning steams with hangovers,
And the clouds are giddy
And beneath them swallows swoop, drunk,
And flowers stagger about on their stems
Drunk on the wind.

Everything in Heaven's too drunk to remember hell.

And the best monsters are drunken monsters,
Trembling and dreaming of beanstalks
Too high for sober Jack to climb,
And the best tightrope walkers are drunken tightrope walkers,
A bottle in each hand they stagger above the net made
Of the audience's wish for them to fall.

Drunk, I've navigated my way home by the blurry stars,
I've been drunk on the future's possibilities
And drunk on its certainties,
And on all its improbabilities I've been so drunk
That logic finally surrendered.

No matter what time it is
No matter where it is
In the room you hate
In the green ditch bloated with spring,
Beside the river that flows
With its million little tributaries
Into a million little graves,
It doesn't matter—
It's time to get drunk.
If one night of oblivion can wash away
All the petty heartache then fine,
Reach for that ancient medicine.

And if you wake from drunkenness
Don't think too much about it,
Don't stop to think.
Don't bother asking clocks what time it is,
Don't bother asking anything that escapes from time
What time it is,
For it will tell you as it runs,
Leap-frogging over all obstacles,
Why idiot, don't you know? It's time to get drunk!
Time not to be the prisoner of bordeom or cemetery stones!
Be drunk on what you want,
Be drunk on anything, anything at all
But please—

Understand the true meaning of drunkenness!

Conversation with a favourite enemy

AT A DINNER party in aid of some unsufferable event
I sit opposite my favourite enemy.
'How's the cabbage?' he smiles.
'Fine,' I say, 'How's your novels?'
Something nasty has started.
On the chicken casserole the hairs bristle.
On the hostess the hairs bristle.
She glances down the dinner table
her eyes eloquent as politicians'.
'Do you find the dumplings to your liking?' she asks,
'Do you find them juicy?'
'Fine,' I say, 'How's your daughter?'
She chokes on the carrot.
After supper the critic's back again,
Wits sharpened on the brandy.
He fold his napkin into the shape of a bird,
'Can you make this sing?' he gloats,
'Would you say it's exactly poetry?'
Ah, but I'm lucky this evening!
In a tree outside a nightingale burst into fragments.
It flings a shrapnel of song against the window.
My enemy ducks, but far too slowly.
It is not always like this.
My enemies are more articulate,
The nightingale, utterly unreliable.

Proclamation from the new Ministry of Culture

A FESTIVAL is to be held during which
A competition is to be held during which
Work that exalts the free spirit of this land
May be submitted.
The judges can be chosen from among yourselves.
The honours to be awarded are numerous,
The prizes to be awarded are numerous.
You may write or paint exactly what you wish,
You may say exactly what you wish
About the free spirit of this land.

Work in bad taste will be disqualified.
Anonymous entries will be ferreted out.
Those who do not enter will be considered
Enemies of the free spirit of this land.

From now on the festival is to be an annual event.

Ghost-culture

THE MINISTER kneeling on the floor hunched over
the home politics page slobbering
pink fingers counting the column inches given
his ghost-written speech on how best
to decapitate the landscape
the hostess
well-feathered house stuffed with finery
the little poet rasping out the tough sonnet
the morose social worker wearing
last year's most expensive fashion
as some kind of penance
the charming young publisher
the charmed financier
the nouveau poor sucking up the atmosphere
the black writer of revolutionary pamphlets
the priest holding forth from the plush armchair
on man's fall from paradise
glib mimic living in light's echo
the neat journalists
the purveyors of wound-cream
the high-class gossip merchants
the sour novelists
the past and present beauties
the landlords of Bedlam
the manipulators of ghost-culture
all history's goblins agile among the contradictions
were stunned into embarrassed silence
when from his pocket the guest of honour
produced a few crumpled and unexplained petals
and wept with exhaustion.

John Poole's bullying the angels

JOHN POOLE'S bullying the angels.
In Paradise the cherubs are shivering with fear,
When his big nasty shadow stomps past
their curls droop.

What's John Poole doing in Paradise,
Smashed on the queer stuff?
How the hell did he get in?
Well, he was that kind of person.

He scared policemen
And loved rabbits and battered women
and loved rabbits.

Maybe that's how he got in.
He loved rabbits more than the cherubs.
He said so, strolling towards Paradise
in a threatening sort of way.

A bird-brained view of power

THE BIRD is paranoiac.
It thinks the leaves are trash piled up around it.
It sings as if it were a criminal,
feeding the silence and then retreating.

Headlights roaming through the trees
Support its delusions.

In the darkness the drab bird broods:
'Surely all this singing is keeping
Important people awake?
Rising from an irritated bed
Tomorrow a Minister will declare war
On some unfortunate province,
And somewhere a tired businessman will make
    The wrong decision and cities
Will be thrown into chaos.'

    In distant mansions
The guard-dogs multiply like rabbits.
God's bigots stalk one another,
Bull-necked or starry-eyed,
They deal in baby-jam.

In the branches the drab bird sings.
Absurd and clichéd as it sounds
In the branches a bird is singing,
singing with mindless persistency
   The one song it knows.
From the night and from antiquity
It has dragged up a single jewel.

Somewhere in a city, in a city
Cordoned by fear,
A fistful of feathers believes
Its song has summoned up demons.
It listens to the wail of sirens.

Headlights roaming through the trees
Support its delusions.

The critics' chorus

Or, What The Poem Lacked

> 'How he got to the point of thinking this sort of thing
> was a poem is a good and appalling question . . .'
> Donald Davie

OF COURSE they were right:
The poem lacked a certain tightness,
Its inventions were chaotic.

In the bleak farmhouse Rimbaud
remembering the jewelled spider webs,
The smoking pond, the banished sideshows.

Of course they were right:
The poems were not fit to be taken seriously,
Mere candyfloss, the efforts of a stablehand.

In Rome coughing up the rose-shaped phlegm
Keats taking the final opiate,
exiled among the fume of poppies.

Of course they were right:
He could have found all he wrote
In the dustbins he emptied.

Where's Hyatt now?
Still drinking the blind wind?
Ghost-junk still flowing in ghost-veins?

Of course they were right:
So much of what she wrote was doggerel,
mere child's play.

In a London suburb Stevie,
Blake's grandchild,
fingering a rosary made of starlight.

Of course they were right:
In all the poems something went astray,
Something not quite at home in their world,
something lost.

It was something to do with what the poem lacked
saved it from oblivion,
a hunger nothing to do with the correct idiom
In which to express itself

but a need to eat a fruit far off
from the safe orchard,
reached by no easy pathway
or route already mapped.

The common denominator

Or, The Ground-Floor Tenant's Only Poem

WHAT ON EARTH are you about?
I've hardly stopped to work that one out.
I don't know why—
I'm about blood of course, and love,
About sex and death,
About fear and half-hearted tenderness—
At a clouded intellect I've hurled
All the clichéd answers in the world,
But mostly it's the day to day
Trivia of getting by
That drains the energy to wonder why
the question's even asked.
Who are you? Where from? And why?
Like a plastic Buddha I have sat
Besuited under mindless trees,
And thinking of the mindless lilies in their fields
I've mused a bit and then
Been confused a bit and then
Still left unsolved such mysteries.
Don't get me wrong—
I'm not convinced there is such a thing
As a wholly complacent man,
All face a private terror now and then,
And nightly through most bedroom walls
Something uninvited crawls.
Who? What? Whither? Why?
I do not know nor very often care,
And as I walk, averagely mindless through the sunny air,
I leave the questions hanging there,
And try my best not to despair.

Brer Rabbit's Howler

BRER RABBIT goes to the ball dressed as a dandy.
He feels good this evening.
Magnanimous towards all creatures, he cannot understand
Why the dancers shy away from him.
What social misdemeanour is it now
That they stiffen at?
He's eaten the lice.
He's washed off the stench of burrows.
The myxamatosis scabs are healed.
What's left to complain about?
He dances to whatever tune's available,
The fox trot, the tango;
His green suit becomes him,
In his lapel
The baby's foot looks charming.

Brer Rabbit in the market place

TODAY THEY'VE been feeding Brer Rabbit.
They've coaxed him down from the hillside,
hidden the furgloves, the rabbit-feet.
The coats worn by ugly women have for today at least
been banned from the market.

'It's Kindness to Rabbits Week,' they explain,
'Skinbag, let's fatten you!
Everyone will want to know you,
Everyone will want to stroke you.
Imagine the comfort!
Imagine the bunnies you could get into!'

Today they are being charitable to Brer Rabbit.
They feed him with lettuce and carrots,
offer fine plates artistically set with flowers.
They show him the most comfortable hutches,
the plastic burrows, the new, grass-free hillsides.
Brer Rabbit doesn't mind.
He eats and says nothing.

He is the one rabbit who will never stay,
who will never grow quite fat enough.
He will be away by nightfall,
when under the glittering kerosene lamps
the fat bunnies are hung and skewered
and all manner of freaks parade between
the meat stalls and the apples.

Brer Rabbit's revenge

SO BRER RABBIT re-enters the burrow.
All day he's been in the world of fantasy,
but now below the drenched allotment
he is at home again.

Through the walls of his burrow rain leaks,
the tunnels turn liquid;
his fur mud-soaked he screams
his hatred of make-believe.

All day he's been bunnying about—
smiling benevolently with the toy shop dummies,
wandering through the nursery
all winsome and innocent.

Now that above ground the children sleep
cocooned in love for him
something drops away and sweetness
is no longer bearable.

Soon enough those children will grow old.
Brer Rabbit climbs into his shroud.
He waits to haunt them.

Brer Rabbit at the ants' banquet

BRER RABBIT sends out messages;
'All's finished here.
In the burrow memory falls away until
There is nothing to cling on to.'
He digs for some image, for some route back
To a time when company existed.
He comes up with nothing.
He watches how frost melts from the apples,
Thinks how the world might be empty, thinks
How old plagues might have settled.
'Once I breakfasted on roses,
I gossiped with tulips,
I invited friends home,
Got them drunk on the brilliant petals!
But then the clouds swarmed,
They sucked up colour. All went.
Blank poppies, small memories of redness.
Little rags, without essence.'
He sniffs the mist to trace a scent,
But there is no difference now
Between enemy and flower.
Daily his brain tightens.
On the leaves he has written his messages;
They darken then vanish.
From the dandelions he has unhooked his longings;
On the wind that changes pollen into dust
They drift, then vanish.
He sinks down the long burrow frightened.

Brer Rabbit changes.
He becomes the ants' banquet,
A focal-point for the flies' reunion.
Into the landscape his brown fur merges.
Soon without fear or shape he will run
Through tunnels of fern and campion,
Down trackways that have for centuries led
From door to green door
Brer Rabbit will be flowing.

Note from the laboratory assistant's notebook

THE DODO came back.
It took off its hat.
It took off its overcoat.
It took off its dark glasses and
put them in its suit pocket.
It looked exhausted.

I made sure the doors were locked.
I turned off several lights.
I got the blood from the fridge
and injected it.

Next I sneaked into the garden and buried
a manuscript containing
The History of Genetic Possibilities.
I washed my fingerprints from things.

I took a bible down from the shelf.
Opening it at Genesis I sat waiting.

Outside, people not from the neighbourhood
were asking questions.

Staring at the crowd

I SAW THE skeleton in everyone
And noticed how it walked in them,
And some, unconscious that Grinning Jack
Abided his time inside their flesh
Stared back, and wondered what I saw.
The way they dressed, a boil on a face,
Their vanities were small and obvious—
Women wore their coldest masks and men
Looked elsewhere and thought perhaps
I was some friend they'd dropped.
But I did not know them well enough to say
It's Grinning Jack I see today,
Not your beauty or your ugliness,
Nor how fresh you seem, nor how obvious
The chemical decay,
But the skeleton that every man
Ignores as calmly as he can,
Who'll kiss us on the cheek and blow
The floss of temporal things away.
It's Grinning Jack I see today,
And once seen he'll never go away.

Song of the grateful char

I'LL SCRUB the doorstep till it blinds you,
I'll polish the candlesticks till they burn,
I'll crawl across the carpet
And suck up all your dirt.

Though the cast-off clothes you gave me
Are much too grand to wear
I'll don them in the bedroom,
And no doubt I'll weep there.

I'll wash the shit from your toilet,
The stiffness from your sheets.
Madam, thank you for employment.
Can I come again next week?

'Sweetheart.' said the banker's wife,
'I too know of despair,
I think about it often
In my house in Eaton Square.'

'Sweetheart,' said the doctor,
'I've no advice today.'
Pain had made him indifferent.
He turned his head away.

Among a pile of nightmares
I heard a woman scream.
'Hush,' said the psychiatrist,
'It is a common dream.'

There are many kinds of poverty,
My mother knows them well.
She sits and counts them in a tenement
A mile or so from hell.

The right mask

ONE NIGHT a poem came to a poet.
From now on, it said, you must wear a mask.
What kind of mask? asked the poet.
A rose mask, said the poem.
I've used it already, said the poet,
I've exhausted it.
Then wear the mask that's made
Out of the nightingale's song, use that mask.
But it's an old mask, said the poet,
It's all used up.
Nonsense! said the poem, it is the perfect mask.
Nevertheless, try on the God mask—
Now that mask illuminates Heaven.
But it is a tired mask, said the poet,
And the stars crawl about in it like ants.
Then try on the troubadour's mask, or the singer's mask,
Try on all the popular masks.
I have, said the poet, but they fit so awkwardly.
Now the poem was getting impatient,
It stamped its foot like a child. It screamed,
Then try on your own face!
Try on the one mask that terrifies you,
The mask no one else could possibly use,
The mask only you can wear out!
He tore at his face till it bled.
This mask? he asked, this mask?
Yes, said the poem, why not?
But he was tired of even that mask.
He had lived too long with it.
He tried to separate himself from it.
Its scream was muffled, it wept,
It tried to be lyrical.

It wriggled into his eyes and mouth,
Into his blood it wriggled.
The next day his friends did not recognize him,
The mask was utterly transparent.
Now it's the right mask, said the poem,
The right mask.
It clung to him lovingly
And never let go again.

Going back and going on

TRYING TO get back before night hid the way
And the path through Sharpham Wood was lost
I still found time to stop, and stopping found
A different path shining through the undergrowth.
It was real enough—
A sun that had been too high to light
The underside of leaves had sunk,
And ground level rays had lit
The tiny roots of things just begun.
Just now begun!
To think on this half-way through what time is left!
Among the dead and glittering brambles on the path
The miracle is obstinate.
There is no 'going back', no wholly repeatable route,
No rearranging time or relationships,
No stopping skin from flaking like a salmon's flesh.
Yet no end of celebration need come about,
No need to say,
'Such and such a thing is done and gone',
The mistake is in the words, and going back
Is just another way of going on.

One reason for sympathy

I RESCUED a bee from a web last night.
It had been there several hours,
Numbed by the cold it could hardly fight
A spider half its size, one programmed
To string a web across the fattest flowers
And transform the pollen into bait.
My sympathy I know now was misplaced,
It had found the right time in which to die.
I saved it while light sank into grass
And trees swelled to claim their space;
I saved it in a time of surface peace.
Next morning as I watched the broken web gather light
Seeing it ruined in the grass I understood
That I had done more harm than good,
And I felt confused by that act
Of egocentric tenderness.
I called it love at first, then care,
Then simple curiosity,
But there was a starker reason for such sympathy.
It is that one day I too will be caught out in the cold,
And finding terror in there being no help at hand
Will remember how once I tried to save a bee—
And hope the same is done for me.

The last gift

For Heinz Henghes

H.H.   'What's the story about?'
B.P.   'About a mouse that gets eaten by an eagle.'
H.H.   'Poor mouse.'
B.P.   'No, the mouse becomes part of the eagle.'
H.H.   'Lucky mouse. Perhaps I'll be that lucky.'

PERHAPS NEXT time he will be
   A musician playing in a hall in which
A few children fidget and dream
While the crowd regrets
What cannot help but pass.
Or perhaps he will be something a snowdrift's buried
And that's not found again,
Or the contradiction of blossom
On a stunted apple-tree.

Perhaps, but all I know for certain
Is that already some friends are in their graves,
And for them the world is no longer fixed
In its stubborn details.
Astonished in moments of clarity to realise
How all that surrounds me has passed
Again and again through death,
I still strut without understanding
Between an entrance of skin and an exit of soil.

It is too much to expect he will come back
In the same form,
Molecule by sweet molecule reassembled.

When the grave pushes him back up
Into the blood or the tongue of a sparrow,
When he becomes the scent of foxglove,
Becomes fish or glow-worm,
When as a mole he nuzzles his way up
Eating worms that once budded inside him,
It's too much to expect that I'll still be around.

I'll not be here when he comes back
As a moth with no memory of flames.

It is a dubious honour getting to know the dead,
Knowing them on more intimate terms,
Friends who come and go in what at the last moment
Seems hardly a moment.
And now as one by dreamless one they are dropped
Into the never distant, dreamless grave,
As individual memory fades
And eye-bewildering light is put aside,
We grow more baffled by this last
Gift of the days they are denied.

Advice from the original gatecrasher to the recently dead

IF YOU ARRIVE outside Paradise and find
entrance is by invitation only and that anyway
from the ledger your name is missing.

do not despair.

At the back of Paradise
in the huge wall that surrounds that place
is a small door;

God and all his angels have forgotten it.

If something goes wrong
and Heaven ignores you,

if what you are is paraded before you and mocked,
do not despair,

you have got too near
for your schemes to be abandoned.

If you are told to go away,
to Hell,
to the blankness already experienced,

you simply sneak round the wall
to the small door at the back of Heaven,

you give it a bit of a push,
and wriggling like a snake
you squeeze yourself in.

And if you ever get hungry no doubt
somewhere you will find an apple tree,
and fruit to share quite generously.

The purpose is ecstasy

BUT IF YOU enter without rapture or without
such hopes as make hoping actual,
you might as well not enter—

'Now' is weighed down by 'ago',
sight's overloaded and the smell
of earth burdened by memory.

What use dragging the body and all
its loose desires and its ghost-connections
through days wounded by doubting,

the purpose is ecstasy—

believe in it, undo the mischief
night's wardens have created.

This is the message I leave myself—
Yet so hard to rise out the trap
of befuddled longings!

Habit hauls in its net,
bulging with Death's cartographers.

Assembling a prayer

SO MANY were spreading darkness as if it were light,
they were broadcasting their sicknesses and their ghosts
hoping they would go, but needing them;
they were digging up the mummified gods
and pulling at their spines to make them gibber.

One of Death's little camp followers
I went along with them chattering sombrely,
my back to the sunlight, arse about face,
my sight permanently fixed in important shadows.

There came a time I believed the future mapped,
that everything was arranged—
except for the daily trivia there seemed
      nothing left to plan,
and though it was still a mystery what route I'd take
and with what cool or lush flesh I'd wake,
I believed what I was was in the blood,
that for good or bad
the chemistry of incident and memory was fixed.

Then I learnt how to throw away the tragic books;
I began ignoring the philosophies that wilted
          at the grave's edge;
the smell of grass became revelation enough.
I needed a new philosophy, a new god, a bright god,
          a light, sun-splashed god.
A god that could gobble up the sickness and the ghosts,
a god that could blow grief away as if grief were a feather.

Out of such longings I have begun to assemble a prayer.

Friends

For Liz Kylle and Harry Fainlight

I MET THEM in bars and in railway stations
And I met them in borrowed rooms and at bright gatherings,
And often enough
I met them with misgivings and doubts,
And misinterpreted what they said
Or did not understand at all, or understood so well
No explanations seemed needed.
And still, for all this, I kept on losing them.

Changes took place, and things that had seemed
Extraordinary and out of reach
Became life's most obvious gifts,
And the world slowed down and I began
To meet them less and less.

Then I learned how the exodus from this place
Is not scheduled,
At times the young leave before the old
And the old
Are left gaping at their fortune.

And now Harry, you too are caught in your own
'Miraculous stream that flows uphill',
Caught up in its flow towards Heaven,
And flesh has dropped away from Love
And bald, bleak memory is all we hold of you.

Looking through an address book containing
The names they have abandoned
I realize that as from today
I haven't fingers enough to count
The graves in which they are exiled.

Something never lost

THERE IS a place where the raspberries burn
And the fat sparrows snore in peace;
Where apples have no fear of teeth,
And a tongue not used to dust
Sings of something never lost;
It is a place not far away.
It takes a lot of trust to reach,
And a spell only love can teach.

The mule's favourite dream

WHEN THE MULE sings the birds will fall silent.
From among them they will choose a messenger.
It will fly to the court of the Emperor
And bowing with much decorum
Will complain bitterly.

And the Emperor, who had long ago banished all cages,
Who until that moment had been astonished
By the birds' flight and by their singing,
Will throw open the windows and listening
Will detect in the mule's song
Some flaw of which he is particularly fond,

And he will say to the bird, 'O stupid thing!
Let the mule sing,
For there has come about a need of change,
There is a hunger now, a need
For different things.'

This is the mule's favourite dream.
It's his own invention.
Deep in his brain's warren it blossoms.

Song about home

I HAVE GONE out, making a pathway through the morning,
Gone out, ankle-deep in silence,
Never to come back this way.
My brain wears a lining of frost, it sparkles,
My way is clear enough.

Call memory forest, and all the things that ever stunned,
The roots of that forest,
Fed by voices so previous
The rain cannot shake them out, nor seasons cancel.
The stars are alive in me,
They go about like drunken satellites.

I'm obsessed, and the obsessions gladden.
I have gone to where the ant goes,
To where the bird whistles.
I follow the vast pathway a snail makes,
Drift unaware through the white dandelions.

Through negligence most friendships have faded,
But what does it matter?
There was never one place I belonged in.
I sing of how home is the place not yet visited,
Built out of longings, mapped out by accidents.

Frogs in the wood

HOW GOOD it would be to be lost again,
Night falling on the compass and the map
Turning to improbable flames,
Bright ashes going out in the ponds.

And how good it would be
To stand bewildered in a strange wood
Where you are the loudest thing,
Your heart making a deafening noise.

And how strange when your fear of being lost has subsided
To stand listening to the frogs holding
Their arguments in the streams,
Condemning the barbarous herons.

And how right it is
To shrug off real and invented grief
As of no importance
To this moment of your life,

When being lost seems
So much more like being found,
And you find all that is lost
Is what weighed you down.